How to Make More Money By Sitting on Your Butt

Yes, the world's greatest investors all agree there are that most of the time doing nothing Is more profitable than doing something.

That's just one of Mark Tier's many conclusions from a lifetime in the markets that contradict the "conventional investment wisdom."

For example. your financial advisor probably suggests diversification as the best investment strategy—because the "conventional" wisdom is that the only way to make big profits in the market is to take big risks.

It's simply not true. Warren Buffett, George Soros, Peter Lynch, Bernard Baruch, Benjamin Graham . . . indeed, all great investors only invest when they are confident they're very unlikely to lose money.

What's more, contrary to what the novice investor believes, their first priority is to not lose money. Making it doesn't even come second!

Inside, you'll also find 7 contrarian investment "tips" from the world's richest investors, how you can avoid being suckered by slick investment marketing, discover your investment edge, and more.

By the same author

MONEY & MARKETS:

How to Spot the Next Starbucks, Whole Foods, Walmart, or
    McDonald's before its shares explode

The Nature of Market Cycles

The Winning Investment Habits of Warren Buffett & George
    Soros: Harness the Genius of the World's Richest Investors

Understanding Inflation

OTHER NON FICTION:

How To Get A Second Passport

When God Speaks for Himself: The Words of God You'll <u>Never</u> Hear in Church or Sunday School (with George Forrai)

Ayn Rand's 5 Surprisingly Simple Rules for Judging Political Candidates: Never be fooled by a politician again!

FICTION:

Give Me Liberty (co-edited with Martin H. Greenberg)

Visions of Liberty (co-edited with Martin H. Greenberg)

Freedom! (co-edited with Martin H. Greenberg)

Trust Your Enemies

See more at marktier.com/my-books

How to Make More Money By Sitting on Your Butt

and other contrarian conclusions from a lifetime in the markets

Mark Tier

inversebooks HONG KONG

Published by Inverse Books
GPO Box 9444, Hong Kong

Copyright © 2017 by Mark Tier
All rights reserved

www.inversebooks.com

How To Make More Money By Sitting on Your Butt was first published in Creating Wealth, November 2015. © 2015 by Mark Tier

The Accountant's Investment Edge was first published in Accountancy Age (UK), March 2006. © 2006 by Mark Tier

A Good Story—but a Good Investment?, *Your Profit is "Virtually" Guaranteed*, *Using Scuttlebutt to Maximize Your Profits*, *Windfall Profits*, and *Contrary to "Contrary Opinion"* first appeared on Mark Tier's blog, Investor's Edge. © Mark Tier 2005, 2006

ISBN: 978-988-78026-5-5

Contents

INTRODUCTION
Can you really make more money by just sitting on your butt?

You bet you can.

Indeed, if you're *not* a "butt-sitting" investor some of the time, you've increased your chances of losing money in the markets.

As legendary trader Jesse Livermore put it: "It was never my thinking that made the big money for me, it always was sitting."

And George Soros: "When there's nothing to do, do nothing."

And Warren Buffett spends most of his time "sitting on his butt"—reading annual reports.

This is just one of the many contrarian conclusions I've come to in the 42 years I've been in the investment marketplace. The following "pages" of this ebook cover ten different topics. And you can find others at my website, *marktier.com*.

Most of these conclusions I've come to the hard way: by losing money or missing out on a slam dunk opportunity.

All in all, an expensive, but ultimately profitable, education.

Let's begin with 7 contrarian investment "tips" from the world's greatest investors...

7 Contrarian Investment "Tips" From the World's Richest Investors

What great investors do that average investors don't

WARREN BUFFETT AND GEORGE SOROS ARE THE WORLD'S richest investors. Their investment styles are as opposite as night and day. Buffett buys companies that he considers to be good bargains; Soros is famous for his speculative forays into the currency markets, which is how he came to be known as "The Man Who Broke the Bank of England."

But—as I have detailed in *The Winning Investments Habits of Warren Buffett & George Soros* (http://marktier.com/harness-investment-genius-warren-buffett-george-soros)—they both practice the same 23 mental habits and strategies religiously. As do Carl Icahn, Sir John Templeton, Bernard Baruch, and all the other successful investors I've ever studied or worked. It doesn't matter whether you buy stocks, short currencies, trade commodities, invest in real estate, or collect ancient manuscripts: adding these mental strategies to your investment armory will do wonders for your bank account.

To make it easy to get going, I've distilled these 23 mental habits into these seven simple (though not always easy to follow) rules:

1. If you're not certain about what you're intending to do, don't do it. Great investors are always certain about what they are doing whenever they put money on the table. If they think something is interesting but they're not sure about it, they do more research—or just take a walk.

So next time, before you call you broker (or go online), ask yourself: "on a scale of 1 to 10, how certain am I that I will make money?" Choose your own cut off point, but if it's less than a 7 or an 8, you definitely need to spend more mental energy before making a commitment.

A cold shower might be even a better "investment."

Remember: the great investor's sense of certainty comes from his own experience and research. If your sense of "certainty" doesn't come from your own research, it's probably a chimera.

2. *Never take big risks*. You probably heard that the only way to make big profits in the market is to take big risks. It's simply not true.

Warren Buffett, George Soros, Peter Lynch…they only invest when they are confident the risk of loss is very slight.

Okay, what about that person you heard about who made a bundle of money in copper or pork belly futures or whatever by taking on enormous leverage and risk?

A few simple questions:

Did he make any other big profits like that?

Did he do this last year as well, and the year before that, and the year before that?

If not, chances are that's the only big profit he ever made.

The great investors make money year in year out. And they do it by avoiding risk like the plague.

3. *Only ever buy bargains*. This is another trait the great investors have in common: they're like supermarket shoppers loading up on sale items at 50% off.

Of course, the stock exchange doesn't advertise when a company's on sale. What's more, if everybody thinks something is a bargain, the chances are it's not (or if it is, it won't be for very long!).

That's how Benjamin Graham, author of the classic *The Intelligent Investor,* averaged 17% a year over several decades of investing. He scoured the stock market for what he considered to be bargains—companies selling under their break-up value—and bought nothing else.

Likewise, Warren Buffett. But his definition of a bargain is very different from Graham's: he will only buy companies he can get at a discount to what he calls "intrinsic value": the discounted present value of the company's future earnings. They're harder to identify than Graham-style bargains. But Buffett did better than Graham: 23.4% a year.

Even George Soros, when he shorted sterling in 1992, was convinced that the pound was so overvalued that there was only one way it could go: down. That's a bargain of a different kind, but a bargain nonetheless.

4. *Do your own leg-work*. How do they find investment bargains? Not in the daily paper: they might occasionally find a good investment idea there, but not any true bargains.

The simple answer to "How do they do it?" is: on *their* own. After all, almost by definition, an investment is only a bargain if hardly anybody knows about it. As soon as the big players discover it, the price goes up.

So it takes time and energy to find an investment bargain. As a result, all the great investors specialize. They have different styles, they have different methods, and they look for different things. That's what they spend most of their time doing: searching, not buying.

So the only way you're going to find bargains in the market is the same way: by doing your own legwork.

5. *"When there's nothing to do, do nothing."* A mistake many investors make is to think that if they're doing nothing, they're not investing.

Nothing could be further from the truth. Every great investor specializes in a very few kinds of investments. As a result, there will always be stretches of time when he can't find anything he wants to buy.

For example, a friend of mine specializes in real estate. His rule is to only buy something when he can net 1% per month. So sometimes he'll sit on his thumbs for years—aside from collecting the rent!

Is he tempted to do something different? Absolutely not. He's made money for decades, sticking to his knitting, and every time he tried something different, he lost money. So he stopped.

6. If you don't know when you're going to sell, don't buy. This is another rule all great investors follow. It's a major cause of their success.

Think about it. You buy something because you think you are going to make a profit. You spend a lot of time so you feel sure you will. Now you own it. It drops in price.

What are you going to do?

If you haven't thought about this in advance, there is a good chance you will panic or procrastinate while the price collapses.

Or...what if it goes up—doubles or triples—what are you going to do? I'll bet you've taken a profit many times only to see the stock continue to soar. How can you know, in advance, when it's likely to be the right time to take a profit? Only by considering all the possibilities.

The great investors all have; and will never make an investment without first having a detailed exit strategy. Follow their lead, and your investment returns should soar.

7. Benchmark yourself. It's tough to beat the market. Most fund managers don't, on average, over time.

If you're not doing better than an index fund, then you're not getting paid for the time and energy you've spent studying the markets. Much better to put your money in such a fund and spend your time looking for that handful of investments you are so positive are such great bargains that you're all but guaranteed to beat the market.

Alternatively, consider the advice from a great trader. When asked what the average trader should do, he replied: "The average trader should find a great trader to do his trading for him, and then go do something he really loves to do."

Exactly the same advice applies to the average investor.

How To Make More Money
By Sitting on Your Butt

WAY BACK IN 1975 RAY, ONE OF MY NEWSLETTER SUBSCRIBERS, called me, all excited.

"I've never made so much money in my life!" he told me.

I knew Ray was a farmer. And while commodity prices had gone up, they hadn't gone up that much. So I wondered what on earth he had done.

"That's the amazing thing," he said. *"Nothing!*

"I sold the farm, put everything in a time deposit—and I'm getting 11.3% by just sitting on my butt!

"More money than I've ever made in 30-odd years of busting a gut on the farm, come rain, hail, or shine."

In the late 1970s and '80s, as you may recall, interest rates world-wide were sky high. In the US, the 10-year Treasury bond paid 10% or more from 1980 to 1985, peaking at 15.32% in January 1981.

In some other countries, rates were even higher. Like Australia, where Ray comes from: interest rates kept rising till 1989, when they peaked at 18.9%!

Today, the era of 10%+ interest rates are long gone.

Nevertheless, I'm going to show you how you can apply the "sitting on your butt" strategy to make more money more easily that you ever thought possible—even when interest rates are 2%—*or lower!*

First, we need to address a couple of seemingly contrarian concepts—entrees, so to speak, before getting to the *chateaubriand.*

When Making a Profit Just Isn't Enough

How do you measure your success as an entrepreneur or investor?

The key, surely, is whether you're making a profit.

Banking a profit certainly means you're not failing.

But in business or investing not failing doesn't necessarily mean you're *succeeding.*

Sound paradoxical? Not really.

For example, too many small businessmen usually work long hours and judge their monetary success on whether they're making a reasonably good income.

But that "income" is really made up of three, very different components.

1. The salary you would have to pay someone to run the business for you; and/or,

2. The market salary the owner should receive for the number of hours he has to put in; and,

3. The operating profit (or loss) *after* those not-so-notional expenses have been deducted.

For example, say you've invested $1,000,000 in your business.

The business is successful in the sense that you're clearing, say, $12,000 a month.

Pretty good income, right?

But—you're putting in 10-12 hours a day, five (or more) days a week to run that business—as the manager.

The median annual salary for a business manager is around $60,000 per year. Or about $30 an hour (for an 8-hour day, 5 days a week).

To calculate your true return on capital, you need to deduct that notional salary.

At $30 an hour, 11 hours a day, 5 days a week, comes to $7,150 per month. That leaves a monthly nett from the $12,000 operating profit of $4,850 a month, or $58,200 a year.

Doesn't sound too bad. Until you realize that's a mere 5.8% return on your million-dollar investment.

An alternative (in the box) produces a return of 6.21%.

Alternatively—

If you've routinized the business you could hire lower paid workers to run it at around $15 an hour. You'd then only need to put in a couple of hours a day supervising, going the bank, and so on.

Here's how that would look:

	Employees	You	TOTALS
Hourly pay	$15.00	$30.00	0.03% to 0.15%
Hours/day	11	2	
Annual wage bill	$60,060	$21,840	$81,900
Operating profit (before wages)			$144,000
Profit after wages			$62,100
Return on $1,000,000 capital			6.21%

Better. But enough?

Not if you can get a similar return by sitting on your butt.

"Opportunity Cost": Could You Make More Profitable Use of Your Time and Money?

When you spend a dollar, your "opportunity cost" is whatever you could have bought instead—but now can't.

A friend of mine used this concept to teach his son about money (like me, he also has a degree in economics, the source of the concept of "opportunity cost." Have to use it somehow!)

Every day the ice cream truck came by. His son's favorite ice cream was 75 cents. An alternative was just 35 cents.

Dad gave him 50 cents pocket money a day. His son had to now choose: save up for his favorite—but have it tomorrow. Or give into his desire for "instant gratification" and buy the cheaper one now—foregoing the possibility of having his favorite the next day.

Similarly, if you've invested $1,000,000 in a business, you're foregoing everything else you could have done with that money. Not to mention what you could have achieved with all that time you're putting in.

To calculate your opportunity cost, let's assume that the stock market's average, long-term return is 9%-11%.

If you'd put that $1,000,000 in an index fund instead, it would produce a lumpy average of around $100,000 a year—while you're just *sitting on your butt.*

Then, instead of putting in 11 hours a day (and spending the rest of the week worrying about the business) you could take a job in a company somewhere as a manager at $30 (or more!) per hour, work a 5-day week—and go the pub at 5pm with an unworried and uncluttered mind.

You'd clear around $60,000(+) per year, with annual and sick leave thrown in (right?).

Total (*average*) annual return: $100,000 + $60,000 = $160,000.

More than the $144,000 the business produces when you put in 11 hour days.

But What About the Sense of Achievement and Fun You Get from Running Your Own Business?

"I'm having so much fun running my business," you might respond, "the last thing I want to do is work for someone else."

I'm with you on that. My last job ended May 1, 1970. Today, I figure I'm totally unemployable. Every day I do stuff for fun when I could make more money doing something else.

So I'm certainly not suggesting you exchange your passion for profits.

And having fun is just one of many possible returns on your investment of time and money. For example: the mouthwatering profits you expect to make when the business really takes off.

Not to mention that big payday when you go public, or some giant conglomerate comes knocking on your door.

What is important is that you know the "opportunity cost" you're paying: what you're foregoing.

Especially as there are plenty of other activities which aren't so much fun, where figuring out your opportunity cost will lead you to making more money more easily than you ever have before.

Next Question: should you devote any of your precious time to investing?

Well, that's your call. But let me show you how opportunity cost might factor into your thinking.

Just like running a business, successful investing requires that you invest your time as well as your money to achieve results. So are you getting a better return on that time and money by investing than you could by doing something else?

To figure that out, we must first establish a "butt-sitting" benchmark so we can measure the opportunity cost of your time and money.

Here are—

Eight "Sitting on Your Butt" Investments

Type	Annual return (as of June 2015)
1. A savings account	0.03%-0.06%
2. Time deposits	0.03% to 0.15%
3. Long term government bonds	2.48% (30-year Treasury bond)
4. Corporate bonds	3.17% (20-year AAA)
5. Dividend-paying stocks	2.10% (S&P 500 dividend yield)
6. An index fund that tracks the market	Around 7% per annum (10 year average)

7. The "Permanent Portfolio"

Developed by Harry Browne, his "permanent portfolio" is divided into four equal parts: cash (at interest), long-term government bonds, gold, and high-beta stocks.

Once a year, the portfolio is typically adjusted back to 25/25/25/25.

Permanent Portfolio, 2004-2015

8. The Millionaire Teacher

Could you become a millionaire on a teacher's salary?

Impossible?

Andrew Hallam did, and explains how in his book, *Millionaire* Teacher.

Hallam divided his savings into two parts. One part in an index fund. The other in bonds. The ratio is age-dependent: at 30, he had 30% in bonds; at 55, 55% in bonds. Adjusted once per year.

Following this strategy, and adding money to his investments every year, turned him into a millionaire.

Time required to manage either of these last two strategies: less than one day per year.

Beating the Benchmark

Figuring out whether you're beating your chosen benchmark is relatively straightforward. "Relatively," because there are so many variables.

Let's take a simple, hypothetical example first to see how it works.

First choose a "butt-sitting" strategy from one of the 8 options above. To keep the maths simple, let's assume a 5% return on your portfolio.

The second assumption: by spending 5 hours a week analyzing the markets, you could triple that return to 15%.

Based on those assumptions, for every $100,000 you have to invest, you'd conceivably make an extra $10,000 a year. Or a touch over $40 for each hour of time you spend on analyzing the market.

Is that the most profitable use of your time?

It depends.

If you're earning $25 an hour, the return on your time is $15 an hour *higher* in the markets.

But if you're a lawyer or other professional who can bill $100 (or more!) an hour, clearly it's more profitable put in that extra hour a day in the office.

The numbers change if your portfolio is larger. If that same lawyer has a million dollar portfolio instead of $100,000, those extra 5 hours a week could add $100,000 a year to his net worth. A return of over $400 an hour.

As you can see, there are quite a few variables. So here's a table that lays them out for two different investment portfolio sizes ($100,000 and $1 million) and two different salary rates ($25 and $100 per hour), with the same assumption that investing 5 hours of your time a week can produce a 15% return in the markets:

As you can see, the higher your salary, the more likely the best return will come from adding an extra hour to your day job.

Comparing your current financial returns to "sitting on your butt" is an important aid to making more money more easily.

So before you embark on any moneymaking endeavor that sucks up either your time or money, consider the alternatives. You might find that the better option is to pour yourself a glass of something interesting and sit back on your butt.

1. $100,000 portfolio; $25 hourly salary

Benchmark	1.50%	2.50%	3.00%	4.00%	5.00%	7.00%	10.00%
Benchmark annual return (per year)	$1,500	$2,500	$3,000	$4,000	$5,000	$7,000	$10,000
Difference @ 15%	$13,500	$12,500	$12,000	$11,000	$10,000	$8,000	$5,000
Return on time (per hour)	$56.25	$52.08	$50.00	$45.83	$41.67	$33.33	$20.83
Per hour difference	$31.25	$27.08	$25.00	$20.83	$16.67	$8.33	-$4.17

2. $100,000 portfolio; $100 hourly salary

Benchmark	1.50%	2.50%	3.00%	4.00%	5.00%	7.00%	10.00%
Benchmark annual return (per year)	$1,500	$2,500	$3,000	$4,000	$5,000	$7,000	$10,000
Difference @ 15%	$13,500	$12,500	$12,000	$11,000	$10,000	$8,000	$5,000
Return on time (per hour)	$56.25	$52.08	$50.00	$45.83	$41.67	$33.33	$20.83
Per hour difference	-$43.75	-$47.92	-$50.00	-$54.17	-$58.33	-$66.67	-$79.17

3. $1,000,000 portfolio; $25 hourly salary

Benchmark	1.50%	2.50%	3.00%	4.00%	5.00%	7.00%	10.00%
Benchmark annual return (per year)	$15,000	$25,000	$30,000	$40,000	$50,000	$70,000	$100,000
Difference @ 15%	$135,000	$125,000	$120,000	$110,000	$100,000	$80,000	$50,000
Return on time (per hour)	$562.50	$520.83	$500.00	$458.33	$416.67	$333.33	$208.33
Per hour difference	$537.50	$495.83	$475.00	$433.33	$391.67	$308.33	$183.33

4. $1,000,000 portfolio; $100 hourly salary

Benchmark	1.50%	2.50%	3.00%	4.00%	5.00%	7.00%	10.00%
Benchmark annual return (per year)	$15,000	$25,000	$30,000	$40,000	$50,000	$70,000	$100,000
Difference @ 15%	$135,000	$125,000	$120,000	$110,000	$100,000	$80,000	$50,000
Return on time (per hour)	$562.50	$520.83	$500.00	$458.33	$416.67	$333.33	$208.33
Per hour difference	$462.50	$420.83	$400.00	$358.33	$316.67	$233.33	$108.33

A Good Story—
but a Good Investment?

Excited about a stock? It pays to remember
Warren Buffett's Investing Rule #1: "Never Lose Money"

W HAT MAKES INVESTORS PILE INTO A STOCK?

The answer to this question was of great concern to a Vancouver stock promoter I met many years ago. After all, that was his business: harnessing investors' greed to sell out his stake in a new company at a juicy profit to himself.

He'd noticed that some newly-listed companies took off, while others with pretty much the same balance sheet and profit and loss statement stagnated or even fell.

By analyzing pairs of such companies, he discovered that the difference that made the difference was the *story*. The company with the sexy sizzle was the one that caught the attention of the media, that got brokers and investors hot under their collars and excited enough to open their wallets.

When he promoted companies like this—even when they had more story than substance—he could bank a handsome profit.

The boring stodgy company—that made bricks, or industrial parts no one had ever heard of—was the one that went nowhere. Even when it was the better investment.

If you pick up any issue of *Forbes, Fortune*, or any other business or investment magazine, you'll find the same principle of "boosterism" at work. And I can't resist using this story from *Fortune* magazine—published during the dot-com boom—to make the point. It begins:

The company that pioneered the trading of natural gas is applying its old paradigm to a newer type of commodity: Internet bandwidth.

The writer quotes several professionals. One said for this company to say "we can do bandwidth trading is like Babe Ruth's saying, I can hit that pitcher. You tell him to get up there and take three swings. The risk is staggeringly low, and the potential reward is staggeringly high." Another applauds its entry into a business she calls "very sleazy—a bunch of cowboys and carpetbaggers."

Then—for a little balance—we hear from two competitors, both skeptical. But the second one adds: "I have no doubt those difficulties will be overcome."

The article concludes by saying that this company...

has resources most dot-coms would die for. In today's environment, where every well-funded tech whippersnapper looks like a genius, it's tempting to root for a graybeard.

As you can gather from these brief excerpts, the entire article exuded great optimism about the future prospects of this company. You couldn't help but believe they were on to a good thing. And the implication was that this new business would generate profits which would drive up the price of the stock.

What was the company? Well, the article came from the January 24, 2000 issue of *Fortune*. And was titled: "Enron Takes Its Pipeline to the Net."

Enron! That's right.

Just after that issue of Fortune came out, Enron raised its earnings estimates and the stock peaked at $81.39 per share. Eleven months later—December 2, 2000—the stock was 40 cents as the company filed for bankruptcy.

Perhaps you think I'm being unfair using this story as an example. And, I admit, it is extreme. But it's not uncommon.

You see, business publications are primarily in the entertainment business. Yes, they contain information. A lot of it good. But their primary aim is to get you to renew your subscription. They achieve that, in part, by serving large dollops of exciting success stories about people and businesses that have made lots of money.

I challenge you to find an issue of business publication *without* such an article.

So next time a report gets you excited about a company, ask yourself: "That's a good story—but would it make a good investment?"

Even in investing the old marketing adage applies: "sell the sizzle, not the steak."

And sometimes there's not even any steak.

Your Profit is "Virtually" Guaranteed

How understanding investment marketing could save you a bundle of money

E VER READ A PITCH FOR SOME INVESTMENT PRODUCT WITH phrases like "your profit is virtually guaranteed," or "you're virtually certain to make money"?

"Virtually" is a great word. In fact, it's my favorite investment marketing word.

Why?

Compare "virtually guaranteed" to, say, "*almost* guaranteed." How interested would you be in an investment that's almost certain to make you money?

Doesn't have the same ring to it, does it? "Virtually" and "almost" have totally different "feels" about them, don't they.

"Virtually guaranteed" has the sense of 99.99999 percent certainty. But if something's only "almost guaranteed" it's more like 50-50 or 60-40 . . . if you're lucky.

Yet if you look up "virtually" in a dictionary, what does it mean? "Almost"!

The English language is rich with synonyms like these, all meaning "virtually" the same thing—but all *feeling* different.

One of the reasons advertising copywriters can make so much money is that they know how to use these synonyms to maximize the emotional impact of their ads. By the time you come to the end of a marketing pitch, if the build-up's been good the words "...and it's virtually guaranteed to make money" slip into your mind as "...and you're *guaranteed* to make money."

Yet has the copywriter told a lie? Of course not! He can simply pick up his dictionary and point out that "virtually" means "almost" or "not quite"...and everybody knows that something that's only almost guaranteed has no guarantee at all.

[Notice how I slipped in the word "only" there? Bet it didn't fully register. But adding that one word makes the sense of "almost" *even more* uncertain than it already is. And putting "almost" in *italics* "virtually guarantees" that your eye will seem to skip over the word "only" entirely. But the implication still sticks.]

Even "tell the truth" laws regulating advertisements don't protect you.

Good marketing tells you the truth, and nothing but the truth.

But it never tells you the *whole* truth.

And if it's *really* good marketing, the emotional impact of the whole can be a wild exaggeration—or even a lie—even though every single statement in the ad, taken by itself, is 100% (not virtually!) true.

So next time you read an ad ask yourself: "Well, that's all very well and good—but what aren't they telling me?"

Answering that one question could save you a bundle of money.

Using Scuttlebutt to Maximize Your Profits

This is a powerful investment tool that requires one major "analytical" talent: the ability to listen

P ROBABLY THE MOST UNDERRATED, AND OFTEN THE MOST rewarding way of testing an investment idea is called "scuttlebutt."

If you haven't come across this term before, it doesn't mean scrounging around in garbage cans (though, come to think of it, that might occasionally be a good idea). It means talking to a number of different people who know something about a company so you can put the pieces together into a comprehensive picture.

Sometimes, it's even easier than that.

For example, my first encounter with the "scuttlebutt" technique was with a Hong Kong company called Giordano.

Despite its Italian name, Giordano is a chain of clothing stores started in Hong Kong by a very interesting entrepreneur named Jimmy Lai. It sells well-made, fashionable clothes very cheaply.

But what intrigued me about this company was that every time I walked into one of its Hong Kong stores, the staff were cheerful, they welcomed you, they didn't hassle you to buy something—but they were always there when you needed help.

While this probably doesn't sound like anything out of the box, in Hong Kong in the 1980s to walk into a shop like this was to experience culture shock.

I mean that literally. Back then, a tourist could go into a camera store loaded with thousands of dollars he intended to spend on expensive gadgets and be met with complete indifference—or worse. Shop assistants in Hong Kong back then made New Yorkers seem like they'd all graduated from charm school—with honors.

My reaction was: *Wow!* If someone can get Hong Kong Chinese shop assistants to act like this, this company is probably a fantastic investment.

So I visited a number of other Giordano stores in Hong Kong, and the experience was exactly the same. I remember reading an article about Jimmy Lai at that time. Apparently, he had no particular interest in clothing or fashion. What he'd done was study successful businesses like McDonald's to figure out how they operated; looked for an empty niche in the market; and created a superbly organized business to fill it.

The story was getting better and better.

Around that time, I travelled to the Philippines and Malaysia. Both these countries are renowned for their happy, smiling people who are always pleased to see you—and even delighted that you've come to visit their country. As it happened, Giordano had expanded into both these countries so naturally I wandered into their stores.

Imagine my surprise when, in both places, I was greeted with reactions varying between complete indifference and outright hostility for disturbing their siesta.

Something in the Giordano model had obviously gone wrong. Clearly, if they couldn't motivate people who are naturally cheerful to be cheerful in their jobs, the investment prospects didn't look so exciting after all.

Not investing in Giordano stock at that time, it turned out, was a very wise decision.

Philip Fisher and Scuttlebutt

Scuttlebutt was the key ingredient in the success of legendary investor Philip Fisher. There's only so much you can learn about a company from reading its annual reports, he once said. To really get to know a company, you've got to get out and talk to people. Not just the company's managers, but its employees, suppliers, retailers and customers. Often, the very best source of information will be the company's competitors. After all, an executive is likely to give you a one-sided view of his own company, but he'll happily tell you anything you want to know about his competitors. Another excellent source is ex-employees, who will no longer be restrained by any loyalties to their former employer.

In his book *Common Stocks and Uncommon Profits* (now considered an investment classic ranked with Benjamin Graham's *The Intelligent Investor*) Fisher talks about the first time he used this approach to evaluate an investment. It was 1928, and radio stocks were hot. So he went and talked to buyers in several San Francisco department stores. They all agreed that Philco radio was the one that was flying off the shelves, while a company which was the darling of Wall Street sold a radio that customers didn't really care much about.

Unfortunately for Fisher, Philco, which was the low-cost manufacturer, was privately-held so he couldn't buy into it. But he was, nevertheless, gratified to watch the stock of the Wall Street favorite sink while the market went to new highs.

The "Thickburger" Turnaround

In early 2003—a more contemporary example—New York-based fund manager *Whitney Tilson* bought stock in a company called CKE Restaurants at $3.49 a share.

A key component of his decision to buy was "scuttlebutt," and 18 months later, the stock was $14 a share—four times higher.

CKE Restaurants then owned the Carl's Jr., Hardee's and La Salsa fast food chains. Whitney was skeptical at first as the company had been in trouble and its brands were sliding in the market. But the management had a turnaround plan which impressed him. Given its financials and so on, the company would be a great buy—if the management's plans paid off.

But would they? And more importantly: how to determine that before everybody else knew about it and the stock was no longer a bargain?

A critical piece of the turnaround plan was the introduction of a new menu in the Hardee's restaurants. And central to that menu was the new "Thickburger," made from Angus beef and selling at a premium price. It was tested in 80 restaurants, and when the test was successful rolled out across the Hardee's chain.

Whitney and a fellow investor spoke to several franchisees, called more than 30 restaurants around the country, as well as visiting stores in different states. They found a consistent story throughout: staff were happier, customers were happier, and most importantly of all, same-store sales in the restaurants with the new menu were mostly up 30%-40%, year on year.

Convinced he was onto a winner he and his friend loaded up—and more than quadrupled their money. Such can be the power of scuttlebutt in digging up information directly from the market that you can be sure hardly anyone else knows about.

[You can read Whitney Tilson's own, more detailed, commentary on this investment and his use of scuttlebutt in the column he wrote for the *Motley Fool*.]

"Call Your Dentist!"

One of my investment coaching clients was interested in a company that is Australia's leading supplier of amalgam—the stuff dentists use to fill your teeth. Or at least, used to use. Nowadays, most dentists use that white filling material that is hardened with ultraviolet light. It's been years since I've had a filling with amalgam.

Something my client wasn't aware of as he hadn't had a tooth filled in years.

So we talked about scuttlebutt and its uses, and at the end of the session I urged him, "Call your dentist."

The next few weeks, every time we talked, I would say, "Have you called your dentist yet?"

Eventually, he reported that his dentist had told him: "Oh, I haven't used that stuff for age. I don't know anyone who does anymore."

While there may have been other reasons for being interested in this company, what attracted my client's attention was its near-monopoly of this niche market. But, clearly, a monopoly in a declining, soon-to-be-nonexistent market is not a recipe for a growth stock. So he lost interest.

Try Your Luck

While it may take more than a single phone call to someone you already know to get the inside skinny on a company, there are always more than one way to skin a cat. Make a list of the sorts of people linked to a company—suppliers, retailers, wholesalers, customers, employees and so on. Then ask yourself if you know anyone who fits into one of those categories—or if you know someone who might know someone who does.

Go to a trade show, go to a company annual meeting, or any other place where the people you would like to talk to are likely to be and try your luck.

Probably the easiest place to do this kind of research is at the retail level. Go into a shop as if you were going to buy something, and ask the sales person all sorts of questions—the obvious questions a customer would ask but make sure you slip in a few important questions like, "Well, which one is the best-selling brand?"

Feeling a little bit nervous about this approach? Pick some product in which you have absolutely no interest. And then go and talk to someone who sells it. If you're not interested, you have no emotional involvement in the outcome, and will find it easier to walk out the door at any time.

The direct approach often works too. Like Philip Fisher, introduce yourself as an investor and explain why you're there and what you want to know. Remember: people love to talk about what they know, and more often than not all they need is a willing audience.

When you've found the right person, there's just one ability you need to use scuttlebutt successfully as an investment tool: the ability to listen.

Windfall Profits

How can you tell when one of your investments has just hit the jackpot?

MANY YEARS AGO I MET A GUY WHO'D DEVELOPED A BACKUP battery to help cars start on cold mornings. Car batteries were nowhere as near as good then as they are now. He figured there'd be a great market in places like northern Europe, Canada and the northern United States where freezing winters often meant cars were hard to start on cold mornings.

The giant battery maker Eveready agreed. They offered him $500,000 for his invention.

Did you ever hear of such a battery? Of course not—because he turned down Eveready's offer. Figured he'd make a lot more on his own... but he never got it off the ground.

A while later I introduced another friend of mine to a stock promoter I knew in Vancouver. My friend had just started a business, had one location in southern California, and planned to franchise it nationwide.

The stock promoter thought it was such a great idea he offered him $5 million on the spot for 50% of the business—with no "due diligence" whatsoever!

Well, to my friend this just confirmed the value of his idea. Positive he could make a lot more money than that, he decided to do it on his own.

Unfortunately, he was very good at *starting* businesses—but hopeless at developing and running them. A year later, he was bankrupt.

At the height of the dot-com boom, another businessman I know was offered $3 million for his company. Convinced it was worth a lot more, he—like my other two friends—turned the offer down.

Unfortunately, his business was in an industry that, ironically, was about to be "disintermediated" by the internet. Today, like the remnants of its previous competition, it's a barely-surviving shell of its former self.

These are examples of what I call "windfall profits." A windfall profit is like winning the lottery. Something completely out of the ordinary happens to drive up the price of your investment—but quickly evaporates if you don't grab it *immediately*.

The question is, can you recognize them when they happen? My three friends couldn't—and they've all regretted their decisions not to take the money many, many times since.

The trap is that you can interpret a sudden jump in the value of your investment as proof of all your expectations. After all, if your stock just doubled more or less overnight, surely this can only mean there's more to come.

Maybe. How can you be certain? After all, the last thing you want to do is to take a profit just because it's there—and then see it double or triple again.

To make the distinction you need to find out *why* your investment has zoomed up. If there's been some dramatic improvement in the business—or if Wall Street has just recognized the value you saw in this company—then maybe there's more to come.

But if the cause is some extraneous factor, then it's probably time to take the money and run.

For example, during the late 1990s' internet boom I owned shares in a company that rented out exhibition equipment...booths, signs, and all the other stuff you see at trade shows. I'd bought it because it was a solid, stable, and *very* boring business that was throwing off steady profits and juicy dividends.

One day I checked the price and noticed that it had gone from a dollar to around $2.50 per share. Unfortunately, a few days earlier it had been over $3.

I quickly found out that the reason for this jump was that the company had been talking—just talking!—to an American outfit about putting its business on the internet.

How could putting up a website suddenly double or triple the number of exhibition booths this company could rent out?

Clearly, impossible.

All that had happened was that the suckers caught up in the "sex appeal" of the internet boom suddenly piled into this stock.

So I called my broker and immediately dumped all my shares. A few months later they were trading at less than I'd originally paid for them. The saddest thing about these windfall profits is that they don't happen very often. I wish I had more than one to talk about.

But I don't.

But I'm certainly ready to grab the next one that comes my way...if it ever does. And I hope you will be, too.

Contrary to "Contrary Opinion"

If there are any shortcuts to wealth, the theory of contrary opinion isn't one of them

T HE THEORY OF CONTRARY OPINION IS APPEALING. THE IDEA that the average investor is usually wrong, operates more on emotion than reason, and often exhibits herd-like behavior is a compelling one with large elements of truth.

Another variation is that professional fund managers aim, primarily, to match each other's performance, so collectively they behave like lemmings—the classic example of self-destructive herd behavior. ("After all," as Warren Buffett put it, "no individual lemming ever got a bad press.") As a result, they offer the perfect "crowd" to bet against.

Wall Street is a favorite whipping boy, so this idea is a staple of investment newsletter marketing, implying the writer has some superior source of information.

Like all myths, the idea of contrary opinion has an element of truth. Legendary investor Bernard Baruch, for example, sold all his stocks while the crowd was frantically buying, shortly before the market crashed in 1929.

In the bear market of 1973-74, Warren Buffett was scooping up shares in the Washington Post Co., paying 20 cents in the dollar, while Wall Street was uniformly of the opinion that the stock "could only go lower."

Jimmy Rogers became famous—and rich—by buying stocks dirt cheap in places like Portugal, Botswana and Malaysia at a time when foreign investing to an American was buying mining stocks on the Vancouver stock exchange. Some 20 years earlier, John Templeton loaded up on stocks in Japan when all the "crowd" knew was that "made in Japan" meant cheap and shoddy.

Yes, great investors usually go against the crowd. They usually buy when others are selling, and sell when others are buying.

But is there any *cause and effect relationship* between their actions and what the crowd is doing? Do you think these great investors ever check out what the average investor is up to—so they can do the opposite?

When he was loading up on the Washington Post Co., do you think Warren Buffett—whose idea of a group decision is to look in the mirror—gave a damn about what Wall Street or anyone else thought?

Put like this, the whole idea of contrary opinion is absurd.

Great investors make up their own minds based on their own—original—research. As a result of *that*, they'll often do the opposite of what the average investor is doing.

But not always.

When George Soros cleaned up by shorting the pound sterling in 1992, he was far from alone. Currency traders know that when the minister of finance announces that his currency won't be devalued, it's usually a sure sign that the writing is on the wall.

In 1992, Soros was one of the "herd" of currency traders betting the pound was about to collapse.

What launched Soros into the limelight was that his profit was $2 *billion*! Compared to "just" the hundreds of thousands or millions that other traders made.

And if anything, the crowd was following him, not the other way around.

Who's consistently wrong?

The other problem with the idea of contrary opinion is that who, exactly, should you be contrary to? Which class of investors—institutions, fund managers, investment advisors, newsletter writers, or "average" investors—is *consistently* wrong?

And if you've figured that out, how do you find out what they're doing so you can do the opposite?

The market is made up of millions of people. There's no way *anybody* can tell with any precision what they're all up to—let alone what they're thinking.

Investment "gurus"—whether major or minor ones—will often give the impression that *they* know. For example, you might read in the newspaper's daily market round up of some analyst saying: "Institutional investors were piling into the market today," or something similar.

How did he know that? We have no idea. What's more, we have no idea if he had any idea!

This is how it works. People want to know *why* something happened: reporting that the Dow went up 30 points or the euro was down 1 cent does not a story make.

So the journalist whose job it is to write this daily commentary flips through his Rolodex of contacts and selects a couple to call for an opinion. "What caused the market/IBM/the dollar to go up/down today?" is the kind of question he'll ask.

The Analyst of the Day will give his explanation. And he won't want to look like a dummy so if he doesn't really know he'll make something up.

I know this is how it works: I've been there, done that.

(The result, of course, is that the explanation given in, say, the *Wall Street Journal* can be the exact opposite of the one you'll find in the *Financial Times* or *Businessweek*.)

And there's the magazine cover "index." Who hasn't heard of the famous *Businessweek* cover announcing the "Death of

Equities"—which ran in 1982, the year the greatest bull market in the history of stock markets began.

Perhaps the *Economist* also tried to make the theory of contrary opinion true. Back in 1998 they ran a cover story titled "Drowning in Oil"—just as oil was bottoming. And a 2004 cover heralded the "Disappearing Dollar"—the exact opposite to the dollar's upsurge over the next four years!

With 20/20 hindsight, it's easy to see these were great "calls" for the contrary opinion aficionado. But what about the other cover stories they ran that were right? They never get mentioned by proponents of the theory of contrary opinion. But you'd have to collate them first before you could rely on any *consistent* inaccuracy.

To try and figure out what "the crowd" is thinking or doing requires lots of research. And if that research is to be sufficiently complete to be accurate it's unlikely to be available until a long time after it's *useful*.

And maybe not even then. Economists and historians are still arguing about the exact causes of the stock market crash in 1929 almost a century after it happened.

Perhaps there is some group of investors or opinion makers— "average" investors, fund managers, institutions, advisors, magazine covers, and so on—which gets it wrong most of the time.

But the reality is rather like a friend of mine put it about a certain investment advisor: "If only he was wrong *all* the time, I could make a bundle of money." Sad to say, if there are any shortcuts to wealth, the theory of contrary opinion isn't one of them.

Why Diversification is one of the Seven Deadly Investment Sins

Diversification. The investment strategy most investment advisors recommend—mainly because they don't know what they're doing

AT FIRST GLANCE, YOU'D THINK THAT GREAT INVESTORS like Warren Buffett and George Soros have little or nothing in common.

Buffett's trademark is buying great businesses for considerably less than what he thinks they're worth—and owning them "forever." Soros is the archetypal speculator, famous for making huge, leveraged trades in the currency and futures markets.

No two investors could seem more opposite. Yet there are a surprising number of mental habits and strategies they both share—traits that underlie their amazing success.

For example, they are both highly risk-averse—but they *never* diversify their investments.

This sounds like a contradiction in terms. Surely, if you don't diversify, you *must* be taking more risk. Doesn't just about every investment advisor, broker and financial planner recommend diversification as the best, if not the only way, you can protect yourself from losing money in the markets?

When Buffett and Soros decide to make an investment, *they always buy as much as they can.* Buffett (net worth from the

Forbes 2013 rich list: $65.4bn) has had as much 35% of his assets in a single stock. Soros ($23bn) sometimes builds speculative positions that exceed his entire net worth. And another great investor, Carl Icahn ($24bn), has on occasion had *all* his assets in just *one stock!*

What's more, analyzing their past investments proves that always buying as much as they can is how they built their incredible fortunes... from nothing.

If they'd practiced diversification, we'd never have heard of them.

How can this be? How come investment professionals—the people who after all should know best—tell us we must diversify, while the world's most successful investors do the exact opposite?

First, let's consider what diversification really means.

Compare two portfolios. The first is diversified among one hundred different stocks; the second is concentrated, with just five.

If one of the stocks in the diversified portfolio doubles in price, the value of the entire portfolio rises just 1%. The same stock in the concentrated portfolio pushes the investor's net worth up 20%.

For the diversified investor to achieve the same result, 20 of the stocks in his portfolio must double—or one of them has to go up 2,000%. Now, what do you think is easier to do:

- identify *one* stock that's likely to double in price; or
- identify *20* stocks that are likely to double?

No contest, right?

Of course, on the other side of the coin, if one of the diversified investor's stocks drops in half, his net worth only declines 0.5%. If the same thing happens in the second portfolio, the concentrated investor sees his wealth drop 10%.

But let me ask you the same question again... which is easier to do:

- identify 100 stocks that are unlikely to fall in price; or
- identify five stocks that are unlikely to fall in price?

Same answer: no contest.

So diversification *is* a great risk-avoidance strategy. But it has one unfortunate side-effect: by its very nature, it's also a great *profit*-avoidance strategy—which is why I call it one of the Seven Deadly Investment Sins.

As *Fortune* magazine once put it: "One of the fictions of investing is that diversification is a key to attaining great wealth. Not true. Diversification can prevent you from losing money, but no one ever joined the billionaire's club through a great diversification strategy."

Fair enough. But the underlying assumption of the adviser who tells us to diversify is that the only alternative is to take too much risk. Which is the certainly the advice they'd give you if—like Carl Icahn—you wanted to put all your money into just one stock.

For a moment, let's move our attention from investors and investing to successful businessmen. Did Bill Gates, for example, start *several* businesses at once to be sure of success?

Of course not! We know almost intuitively that if someone is going to build a successful business, he has to focus on just that business and nothing else pretty much 24 hours a day for ten, even twenty years. And that if he started out with two or three different businesses, he'd fail at every one for sure.

It's quite true that most new businesses fail. But every business consultant advises their clients to not even think about entering a second business until, at the very least, they've made their first business successful. Furthermore, they all stress, success depends on focusing their *attention* and *concentrating* their energies in as narrow a field as possible.

And that's exactly what the great investors do.

One other thing to keep in mind is that for the Buffetts and Soroses of this world, investing is their bread and butter—and their life's work. To them taking a loss, no matter how small, is like taking a pay cut: something to be avoided at all costs.

So their *first* aim is always to avoid risk, and they work hard to ensure that for every one of their investments, their risk of loss is minimal to non-existent. Only *then* do they worry about profits.

How can they be risk-averse, yet never diversify? By using four other methods of risk-control that your Wall Street advisor has probably never heard of—but are far more effective than diversification.

Warren Buffett, for example, waits until he finds an investment that, to him, is a bargain. When he finds a company he can buy at 50 to 75 cents in the dollar, he acts like the supermarket shopper who sees her favorite soap on sale at 50% off and loads up her trolley with as much as she can.

"You Call That a Position?"

Soon after he took over management of the Quantum Fund from George Soros, Stanley Druckenmiller shorted the dollar against the German mark. The trade was showing a profit when Soros asked him, "How big a position do you have?"

"One billion dollars," Druckenmiller answered.

"You call that a position?" Soros said, a question that has become a part of Wall Street folklore.

Soros prompted him to double his position.

"Soros has taught me," noted Druckenmiller, "that when you have tremendous conviction on a trade, you have to go for the jugular....It's not whether you're right or wrong that's important, but how much money you make when you're right and how much you lose when you're wrong.

"As far as Soros is concerned, when you're right on something, *you can't own enough.*"

Which is exactly what Buffett does when he finds a company "on sale" at 50% off.

Of course, unlike your neighborhood supermarket, the stock market never runs an ad to tell you when a company is on sale at a bargain price.

The great investor has to find such bargains himself. So he spends nearly all his time and energy searching for opportunities that he is sure *will* make him a bundle of money with minimal risk.

Investments like these are very difficult to find. Who knows when he'll come across the next one? What's the point in sitting on a pile of cash waiting for an opportunity that may be a long time coming when, right now, he can see piles of money sitting on the table, begging to be scooped up?

That's why when Buffett and Soros buy, they buy big.

To quote from another legendary investor, Bernard Baruch:

> *"It is unwise to spread one's funds over too many different securities.* Time and energy are required to keep abreast of the forces that may change the value of a security. While one can know all there is to know about a few issues, one cannot possibly know all one needs to know about a great many issues."

Or as Warren Buffett puts it: "Diversification is a protection against ignorance. [It] makes very little sense for those who know what they're doing."

The Accountant's Investment Edge

Accountants have nearly all the tools they need to be GREAT investors. If only they knew it

BALANCE SHEETS CAN TELL ALL KINDS OF INTERESTING STORIES.

A friend of mine once asked me what I thought of a company he worked with. I did some digging and the next time we met, I asked him: "Is the boss sleeping with his secretary?"

"How did you figure that out?" he asked me.

"Well," I told him, "according to the latest annual report, a woman whose job description is 'secretary' is getting an enormous salary, plus stock options and all kinds of other benefits. IBM could hire a high-powered executive for what she's getting paid."

Nuggets of Gold

Not all companies have such scandalous tidbits hidden away in the fine print. But the ability to read a balance sheet and a profit and loss statement—especially if you can read between the lines—is a powerful way to dig up listed companies with hidden nuggets of gold. And just as importantly, weed out the dross.

It was these tools that the legendary investor, Benjamin Graham—author of the classic investment primer, *The Intelligent Investor*—used to build his fortune. These same tools are major weapons in the armory of his star student, Warren Buffett.

Graham analyzed companies' annual reports to find stocks that were selling below their intrinsic (or "break-up") value. He didn't visit company managements; he didn't even want to know what products the companies sold; he was only interested in the numbers.

Of course, there is a danger in this approach. Often, a company's stock is selling below its net worth for very good reasons. Maybe it's just because the market has hammered it down. But perhaps the industry is in decline, the management is incompetent, a new competitor with a superior product is decimating the company's sales...there are a host of possibilities.

By solely relying on annual reports, Graham had no idea *why* a company was cheap. So he could—and did—buy stocks that declined, taking a loss.

Nevertheless, his investments returned profits of 17% a year, on average, over several decades.

How did he achieve this when, clearly, some of the stocks he bought turned out to be dogs?

He bought a large number of cheap stocks, knowing that while he'd lose money on some of them, he'd make more money on the rest.

To help ensure that outcome, he'd only buy companies with histories of steady management, rising profits and regular dividends. All information you can find in annual reports.

This would weed out many (though not all) of the companies that were cheap because they deserved to be.

And he had another, crucial rule: he would only buy a stock selling for less than half its liquidation value, which he called his "margin of safety."

Stocks like that are a lot harder to find today than they were in the 1930's, 40's and 50's when Graham was active. But not impossible: Walter Schloss, a contemporary of Buffett's who was also a Graham disciple, continued to follow Graham's style with great success until he retired in 2002 at the age of 85.

Clearly, mastery of an accountant's tools are essential for anyone who wishes to successfully invest in stocks.

But if that is all you needed, you wouldn't be able to hire an accountant for love or money. They'd all be sunning themselves in the south of France watching their investment profits roll in.

So why haven't more accountants retired from keeping other people's books in favor of "clipping their own coupons"?

Two main reasons.

Few of them realize that unravelling the secrets hidden in an annual report are an essential talent for anyone who wants to identify a great investment—and that they already have all those necessary skills at their fingertips.

But—to turn those insights into market profits also requires a complete investment system: a method or a set of rules that tells you what to do once you've found an investment that looks promising.

And for those of us who aren't accountants and (let's be honest) don't want to be?

After all, our real interest is not accounting but investment valuation. So why not start with the man who so applied all these "accounting" tools to valuing investments so successfully: Benjamin Graham and his classic, *The Intelligent Investor*? After which you might consider "graduating" to his *Security Analysis*.

No need to reach for any of those dry and dusty accounting textbooks after all.

What's Your Investment Style?
"Know thyself" is one of the secrets of investment success

E VERY SUCCESSFUL INVESTOR HAS HIS OWN APPROACH THAT
suits his personality. Warren Buffett, for example, began
his investing career in the 1950s as a Benjamin Graham "clone"
(see more on Graham's style in *7 Investment Tips From the
World's Richest Investors*). Today, while some of the criteria he
applies today are different from Graham's, he still aims to buy
below intrinsic value. But he now defines intrinsic value as the
discounted present value of a company's future earnings, not its
break-up value, which was Graham's metric.

Sir John Templeton is also a former Graham student. But he
didn't just look for the cheapest stocks in the United States; he
searched for the cheapest stocks in the entire world, and made
a fortune for himself and his investors in the process.

George Soros—whose success owes nothing to Graham or
Buffett—has an entirely different and speculative approach.
Even so, Soros's investment system is composed of the same 12
building blocks as Graham's and Buffett's.

What's more, so are the investment approaches of Bernard
Baruch, Carl Icahn, Peter Lynch, Philip Fisher and all the other
successful investors I've studied and worked with.

Even successful investors in real estate, antiques and
collectibles, not to mention commodity and currency

speculators—totally different markets—owe their success to having a system comprised of the same essential elements—one that fits their personality and interests.

Do you know what your investment style is? The simplest way to find is to answer my *Investor Personality Profile* questionnaire (marktier.com/ip). And while you're there, compare your *Investment IQ* with Warren Buffett's, George Soros', and Carl Icahn's (marktier.com/iq). You'll receive a detailed analysis of your strengths and weaknesses—and how to turn those weaknesses into strengths.

ABOUT THE AUTHOR

Mark Tier, an Australian based in Hong Kong, started writing when he was 14—and hasn't stopped since.

His first work, *Understanding Inflation*, was a bestseller in his native Australia in 1974. That was followed by *The Nature of Market Cycles*, *How To Get A Second Passport*, and *The Winning Investment Habits of Warren Buffett & George Soros*, which has been published in 3 English (New York, London, & Hong Kong) and 11 other-language editions.

Once labelled "the Eclectic Investor" for his wide range of interests (he has been a soldier, businessman, publisher, investment analyst, counsellor, coach, writer, investor, speaker, editor, foreign correspondent, and even co-founded a political party), he co-edited two science fiction anthologies, *Give Me Liberty* and *Visions of Liberty*, which won a Prometheus Award in 2005, an analysis of Christianity, *When God Speaks for Himself*, a political thriller, *Trust Your Enemies*, and *Ayn Rand's 5 Surprisingly Simple Rules for Judging Political Candidates*.

See more at *marktier.com*

Preview How to Spot the Next Starbucks,
Whole Foods, Walmart or McDonald's
—before its shares explode

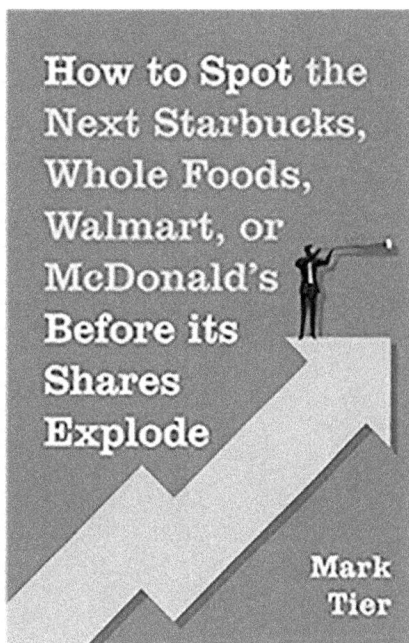

The Differences That Make the Difference

Why does Starbucks have more stores than any other coffee company, and not Peet's (which had a 20-year head start on Starbucks), Seattle's Best, or someone else?

➤ What turned an "upstart" discounter named Walmart into the world's biggest and most profitable retailer, and one of the world's top two companies by sales?* In the process, passing the then much larger Kmart and Target chains to become bigger than both of them combined?

➤ How come Ray Kroc's McDonald's gained the "First Mover" advantage, to become the world's biggest hamburger chain, while Burger King, which had a two-year head start, lost theirs? And a third burger chain, Burger Chef, which was within shooting distance of taking the #1 spot from McDonald's—went out of business instead?

➤ And why was Whole Foods, of the hundreds of specialty grocers in the United States when it opened its doors, the one that grew to dominate its market?

What, to summarize, are the *crucial differences that make the difference* between a good company and a great growth stock?

These are the questions that we'll be examining—and answering—here. The aim is to give you the tools and concepts you need to identify the next startup company that could follow in the footsteps of these four.

Tools that can *also* be applied to start the "Next Starbucks" yourself.

And with numbers like these, who wouldn't want to get in on the ground floor?

	McDonalds	Walmart	Whole Foods	Starbucks
	Value of $1,000 invested at the IPO of			
IPO date	21 April 1965	1 October 1970	23 January 1992	1 June 92
$1,000 invested at IPO now worth†	$3,705,110.93	$8,637,595.15	$26,757.65	$201,901.18
Dividends	$6,438, 828.27	$1,526,522.10	$3,913.39	$4,023.25
Total return	$10,143,939.20	$10,164,117.26	$30,671.04	$205,924.42
Compounded annual return	19.6%	22.2%	14.8%	24.5%
S&P 500	6.38%	7.27%	6.85%	7.10%

* Every year since 2000, Walmart and Exxon have shared the top two spots on the Fortune 500 list, alternating (mostly) with the price of oil.

† As of 26 October 2016. S&P comparison over same time period as each company's IPO to present. *Sources:* Yahoo Finance, walmart.com, aboutmcdonalds.com.

By comparing Starbucks' pattern of growth to that of other high-growth companies we can single out the five significant factors they *all* have in common. The practices that made Starbucks, McDonalds, Walmart, Whole Foods and their ilk tower above their many competitors.

Once we've identified the "differences that make the difference," they become:

The 5 Clues to Spotting the Next Starbucks

- **They _Permanently_ Change People's Habits:** McDonalds permanently changed the way we eat—indeed, McDonalds kicked off the fast food business as we know it today. Walmart and Whole Foods changed the way people shop; and before Starbucks, how many Americans had heard of a $4 latte, let alone drunk one?
- **They're Copycats:** Ray Kroc duplicated the original McDonald brothers' store worldwide—lock, stock, and barrel.
- **Their Success is Validated by Competition:** There are thousands of Starbucks, McDonald's, Walmart, and Whole Foods "clones" around the world—with more opening just about every day. Competition proves the founder's concept, and demonstrates that the potential size of the market is enormous. A company that does not inspire competition is destined to serve a small market niche.
- **They're Driven by the Founder's Vision and Passion:** A company whose management doesn't inspire its employees won't inspire—and *keep*—its customers. The founders of Starbucks (Howard Schultz), Whole Foods (John Mackey), Walmart (Sam Walton), and McDonald's (Ray Kroc) all successfully transmitted their vision and passion throughout their companies, translating it into a unique customer experience.
- **They have Superb _Entrepreneurial_ Management and Execution:** Thousands of good to great businesses share the first four characteristics, but without entrepreneurs at the helm who also have superb management and execution skills, they're destined to remain small, or even one-man bands.

None of these factors is necessarily unique to a growth company. But when you find all five together in *one* company, you can be pretty confident that you've found a great candidate for the next high-growth stock.

But how can you, as an "average-investor-in-the-street," find such a hot growth stock? Especially when you have no access to top management, no insider information and no hope of getting any, and would rather go to Starbucks than read its annual report?

While it's not easy, it's a lot easier than you probably think.

The first step is to appreciate how and why companies that faithfully practice the "5 clues" inevitably outstrip competitors that don't.

This is the subject of Part I, where we compare Starbucks, McDonalds, Walmart, and Whole Foods with each other—and with their various competitors that fell behind—to see exactly how and why the 5 clues separate a great company from a merely good one.

In Part II, we apply the resulting framework to see how it is possible to identify a great company—when it is still small.

You'll end up with detailed techniques you can apply to spot a high-growth stock—and, just as importantly—strike the "Next Turkey" off your list.

You'll also discover—

> ➤ Nine ways to spot the "Next Starbucks" by just "walking around"
> ➤ How you can apply the "5 clues" to dig up hidden gems and beat the Wall Street "experts"—from the comfort of your own home
> ➤ Four completely different ways to profit from the next hot growth stock—or the last one
> ➤ How to weed out the dross by "reading between the lines" of a company's annual report—even if the last thing you'd want to do is take Accounting 101.
> ➤ And—paradoxically—you'll also learn there will be times when you can make more money more easily by investing in the *last* Starbucks (or one of its competitors) not the next one.

Applying the "five clues" to identify the next growth company has a surprising side-effect: identifying the "ingredients" essential for a small business to become a big one becomes a "recipe" for starting a successful business of your own.

Which means: rather than investing in the "Next Starbucks," you could decide to create it yourself!

1 Why aren't there any Starbucks stores in Italy?

Starbucks opened its first European store in 1998—in the UK.

Today, the only countries in Western Europe without a Starbucks are the small and mostly poorer markets of Albania, Bosnia, Croatia, Liechtenstein, Macedonia, Malta, Serbia, Slovenia.

And Italy.

Which is where Starbucks, as we know it today, began, back in 1983. As *Businessweek* put it: "If it weren't for Italy, Starbucks might not exist."[1]

The first Starbucks outlet in Italy will open in 2018. Twenty years after Starbucks first crossed the Atlantic.

What took them so long?

This hardly seems like the first question that would come to anyone's mind. Yet the answer is the key to understanding Starbucks' success, some of its failures—and how it has permanently changed people's coffee-drinking habits. As Howard Schultz relates the story in his book, *Pour Your Heart Into It: How Starbucks Built a Company One Cup at a Time*,[2] he was in Milan on business. He was marketing director of Starbucks, at that time a Seattle-based coffee roaster and retailer of coffee beans. There, "I discovered the ritual and romance of coffee bars in Italy."[3]

Clue #1: Permanently Change People's Habits

When you see a product like the computer, which has replaced typewriters, low-cost airlines that attract people who've never flown before (not to mention rich cheapskates), and innovations like the Tetra-Pak which replaces plastic and glass bottles and containers—and has revolutionized the shipping industry—you know you could be onto the next "big thing."

Inspired by what he saw, Schultz spent his spare time in Milan wandering through the streets and piazzas, observing customers, baristas, and sampling espressos at a handful of the 1,500-odd coffee bars in Milan back then.

It seemed they were on every street corner, and all were packed....My mind started churning....

> As I watched, I had a revelation: Starbucks had missed the point—completely missed it....What we had to do was unlock the romance and mystery of coffee, firsthand, in coffee bars.[4]

Schultz returned to the United States with the vision of what would eventually become Starbucks as we know it today: a fusion of Italian espresso café culture with a McDonald's-style operating model.

Vainly, he tried to persuade his employers to expand into espresso bars. Despite repeated rejection, Schultz was persistent. When Starbucks opened a new store in downtown Seattle, he was offered a small corner for an experimental coffee bar.

It was a success.

Nevertheless, Starbucks' management decided to "stick to its knitting" and not embark on a brand extension. So Schultz quit to pursue his dream, starting *Il Giornale* in honor of the Milan espresso bars which inspired his epiphany.

From the beginning, Schultz was aiming high: *Il Giornale* stores all over the US, if not the world. When his former employer came up for sale Schultz had five *Il Giornale* stores: three in Seattle, plus one in Vancouver and another in Chicago.

Why Vancouver and Chicago, when it would have been easier, not to mention more economical, to open stores closer to home? Schultz wanted to prove to his investors (and himself) that his concept would travel, whetting their lips for the profits to be had in a nationwide chain.

In retrospect, Schultz's 1987 purchase of Starbucks was a stroke of genius. After all, "Il Giornale" was *not* an Italian espresso bar, but an American one. Added to which, for too many Americans, "Il Giornale" was unpronounceable.

Changing the company's name to Starbucks was an unexpected bonus to the obvious fit of having an in-house coffee roaster experienced in sourcing high-quality coffee beans from around the world.

Eleven years later with 1,412 stores in the US and Canada, Japan, Singapore, and the Philippines, Starbucks began expanding into Europe. The UK was the first stop, but Italy was one of the countries on the list.[5]

Yet, today, as I write these words, there's not a single Starbucks in Italy.

Why not?

We can find the answer some 9,000 miles away in Australia, almost on the other side of the globe.

In 2008, for the first time since it was founded, Starbucks shrank. It closed underperforming stores all over the world. The most, 661, were in the United States. But the worst-hit country was Australia, where 61 of Starbucks' 84 stores disappeared.

What went wrong in Australia?

To start with, Starbucks was nothing new.

I'm Australian, and I had my first cappuccino as a university student in the late '60s. It was in a coffee shop called Gus's Café in Canberra, Australia's capital.

Started by a Viennese named Gus, he'd fought city hall for the right to place tables outside, on the sidewalk. We students cheered him on, if only to give the local government a bloody nose. It became one of our favorite hangouts.

Gus was one of many European immigrants—from Italy, France, Germany, Greece, and Austria—who brought the continental coffee culture to Australia after the second world war.

Gus's Café

The history of Gus's Café (from its website,[6] which accords with my memory) sounds rather like the experience of Howard Schultz some 16 years later:

> Canberra's thriving, cosmopolitan café society owes much to the perseverance and vision of one unique individual—Augustin "Gus" Petersilka (1913-1994). A Vienna native, Gus brought the concept of the continental-style café with him to the nation's capital. His idea was simple, yet radical, for its time—the promotion and cultivation of a relaxed and convivial outdoor dining environment in the heart of the city.

> However, turning this dream into reality didn't come easily and Gus's epic battle with local bureaucrats and council officials (including a petition to the Queen) is now legendary. Gus' passion and determination resulted in the opening of Canberra's first open-air, late night café in 1968

The result is that today you can get a great cappuccino, espresso, or latte just about anywhere in the country. And I mean *anywhere*. The best cappuccino I've ever had was in some small country town I drove through on the way to somewhere else. I can't recall the name of the café. Or the town, which was about 200 miles northwest of Sydney with a population of a couple of thousand people.

The selection of this café was pure chance: a pleasant-looking place to take a break. The superb (compared to the usual good-to-excellent) cappuccino was a surprise bonus.

Long before Howard Schultz had his epiphany in Milan, Australia was, like Italy, "cappuccino country."

When Starbucks opened up in Australia, it brought nothing new or different. And certainly not better.

But in the United States, the UK, Canada, and many other countries Starbucks flourished. For espresso, these countries were—

Virgin territory

In 1976 I went to graduate school at UCLA. (I quickly dropped out, but that's another story.) Back then, the best coffee you could get was the stuff that had been sitting on a hotplate for half an hour. Unless you made drip-coffee at home. If there was an espresso available anywhere in Los Angeles back then, I never heard of it.

Returning to Australia from LA, I stopped in London. The coffee there was even worse. (And let's not talk about the service: "execrable" fails to describe how dismal it was.)

Neither the US nor the UK had an "espresso culture."

Howard Schultz's epiphany in Milan was (with the benefit of hind-sight) very simple:

If Italians like sitting around in cafés sipping espressos, so will Americans.

His test with Il Giornale confirmed his insight. And Starbucks' expansion around the world—generating hundreds if not thousands of competitors—proves it conclusively.

But not yet in Italy. Indeed, with the exception of New Zealand and Switzerland, Starbucks has limited penetration in espresso-culture countries, measured by the number of stores per million people:

Country	Number of Starbucks stores	% of all Starbucks stores	Stores per million people
US	13327	64.44	42.2
Canada	1437	6.38	41.1
Singapore	125	0.39	23.5
Taiwan	380	1.38	16.3
UK	884	3.89	14.0
Japan	1191	4.8	9.3
Malaysia	220	0.65	7.4
Hong Kong	50	0.62	7.0
Thailand	264	0.81	4.0
Saudi Arabia	90	0.32	3.2
Philippines	283	1	3.1
China	2309	3.59	1.7
India	83	0.01	0.1

Espresso culture countries

Switzerland	52	0.26	6.5
New Zealand	25	0.17	5.6
Netherlands	59	0.13	3.5
Austria	18	0.06	2.1
Germany	161	0.8	2.0
France	121	0.4	1.8
Australia	23	0.12	1.0
Italy	0		0

As of 7 July 2016. Source: http://www.loxcel.com/sbux-faq.html, Starbucks Hong Kong, http://www.starbucks.com.hk/store-locator/search

Virgin territories are far more profitable. Which explains why Starbucks has the most stores *per capita* in countries like the US, Canada, Hong Kong, Singapore, and Taiwan, where it *changed people's habits*.

Even non-espresso markets like Malaysia, Thailand, and the Philippines, where *per capita* incomes range from 21% (Malaysia) to a mere 4.9% (Philippines) of the US, can be more profitable than Italy (per capita income: 75% of the US). As the table shows, Starbucks has a higher penetration rate in these three countries than it has in any continental European country, other than Switzerland and the Netherlands.

And, to come, are the markets with the most long-term potential of all: China and India. Already, Starbucks has more stores in China (2,309) than it has in the whole of continental Europe, *plus Russia* (1,775)! With the same penetration rate as the Philippines (2.9 stores per million people) Starbucks could have around 7,500 stores in China and India, over half the US number. And in the long run, *both* markets could be way bigger than the US.

Compare that to Italy's potential: with the same penetration as France (1.7 per million), about 102 stores. Easy choice.

Schultz *changed people's habits,* turning drip and instant coffee drinkers into espresso drinkers, by the millions—when *Starbucks entered virgin territory.*

While Starbucks is certainly the most spectacular recent example of this phenomenon, it is merely the latest entrant in what we can term—

Australia's Espresso Culture

The simplest way to understand the hold espresso has on Australian coffee drinkers is to visit the sleepy country town of Armidale, 500 kilometers north of Sydney. Population: 25,000.

In Armidale's downtown area—the size of a handful of New York City blocks—are twenty coffee cafés. There are seven more in other parts of town—without counting the McCafé!

That's more than one café per thousand people.

Assuming this represents total market saturation, it suggests the maximum limit for espresso cafés is 1,120 per million population—comparable to Milan's 1,154 per million people around the time Howard Shultz had his epiphany.

Compare that to the current 70.3 cafés per million people in the US, or 160.9 in the UK: even if you cut the high Australian and Italian numbers in half or to a quarter, the espresso revolution obviously has a long way to go in these other countries.

The Aussies Are Coming. "I often have to explain to people that the best coffee you can get is in Australia," writes Heston Blumenthal in *The Guardian*. "They can't quite believe it. It's starting to happen in the UK and there's some great emerging coffee in Scandinavia, but they are not inspired by Italy, they are inspired by Australia."[7]

The Wall Street Journal agrees: "While many people think Australia's favorite brew is beer, the country is perhaps equally obsessed with coffee.... Specialty cafés are being opened across the city [of New York] by a wave of young Australian entrepreneurs who want to change the way New Yorkers drink coffee."[8]

The McDonald Brothers' Fast-Food Revolution

The restaurant business before McDonald's was like the car industry before Henry Ford's Model-T. Cars were made in small production runs or even hand assembled, one at a time, by skilled craftsmen. They were expensive, often unreliable, and only the wealthy could afford them.

The Model-T was the world's first mass-produced automobile. Introduced in 1908, it cost $950, less than half the price of the average auto. It sold 10,000 units in its first year.

By 1920 the price had fallen to $280: as Ford refined his production techniques, he passed his lower costs to his customers. When the last Model-T came off the production line, 15 million had been sold and over half the cars in the United States were Model-Ts.

Ford's innovations revolutionized the automobile business, and were quickly copied by other manufacturers. As a result, cars became a mass market consumer good rather than a niche product reserved for the wealthy few.

In 1948—40 years after the Model-T's introduction—brothers Richard ("Dick") and Maurice ("Mac") McDonald set in motion a similar revolution in the restaurant business.

By offering a limited, self-service menu of burgers, fries, soft drinks, and shakes, they made eating out an affordable experience for just about everyone.

Today, we think nothing of taking the kids to McDonald's or one of its many clones. But in 1948, for the majority of people a visit to a restaurant was a special occasion, mainly reserved for birthdays, anniversaries, and the like.

The major change that helped drive the growth of McDonald's and similar chains was the postwar boom that slowly eroded people's "Depression mentality." From conversations I've had with American friends in their late 60s, even when their parents graduated from the poor to the middle class, they continued their Depression-inspired habits of rarely eating out.

It was the next generation who were happier to spend rather than skimp. And this happened at the time the McDonald brothers dramatically cut the price of eating out. Their hamburger cost just 15¢, *half* the price charged by most other vendors.[9] They achieved this dramatic price reduction by—

- Limiting choice to just four items: burgers, fries, soft drinks, and shakes, compared to the standard restaurant menu which can run to a small book. Rather than holding inventory to make twenty or a hundred different dishes, they needed to stock only for four.

- As a result, they could apply Henry Ford's assembly line concept to the preparation of food. Instead of cooking one meal at a time, they had special equipment made by a local craftsman that cooked two dozen burgers at once, while another machine prepared the same number of buns. Production was broken down into components: frying the patties, preparing the buns, assembling the burger, preparing the fries and drinks—with countermen to serve the customers. As a result, qualified cooks could be replaced with unskilled workers. And as a self-service restaurant, no waiters were needed.

- They also cut the startup cost. In the 1950s, a McDonald's-style restaurant could be set up for around $75,000, *including* land and building, compared to $300,000 and up for other restaurants.[10]

- Overall, they dramatically cut the cost of production, passing the savings to their customers: McDonald's 15 cent hamburgers attracted buyers in droves.

Today, we take this for granted. But back then the whole world was virgin territory for their concept.

Other restaurateurs, mostly in California, quickly copied their low-cost production methods. Fast food chains like Taco Bell, Kentucky Fried Chicken, and Burger King all had their beginnings in the late 1940s and early '50s—inspired by the McDonald brothers' store.

But most of the copycats strayed from the brothers' concept in one or more ways. Some expanded the menu, others charged higher prices, and few of them reached the McDonald brothers' standard of efficiency and cleanliness.

Until Ray Kroc came along and turned the McDonald brothers' fast-food revolution into a nationwide, and later global, phenomenon.

The McDonald's Revolution, Part II

In 1954, Ray Kroc signed an exclusive nationwide franchise deal with the McDonald brothers, and opened his first store in April 1955 in Des Plaines, Illinois. He "cloned" the original store, maintaining (and eventually improving) the brothers' highly efficient production methods, limited menu, and affordable prices.

Stretched for capital, he turned to franchising and—as we'll see in Chapter 5—developed a highly profitable franchising method which was also very affordable to the franchisee. It also enabled him to maintain a tight control on the quality of franchisees' operations resulting in a high standard of consistency across different stores. A consistency we now take for granted that was unusual at the time.

Thus, he invented the franchising model that's virtually universal today. When Kroc started out, franchisors made their money from *selling* franchises: few of them paid much attention to whether franchisees maintained standards, flourished—or went out of business. To Kroc, his franchisees were his business *partners*: they swam or sank together. Kroc's profits came from the same source as his partners': *customers*.

McDonald's took off: by 1972 it was the world's biggest restaurant chain by sales, a position it has held every year to this day.[*]

To appreciate the magnitude of the "McDonald's revolution," imagine for a moment a world with no McDonald's, no Burger King, no Pizza Hut, no Kentucky Fried Chicken, no Taco Bell, none of their many competitors, and no other fast food chain inspired by the McDonald's model. Not even a Starbucks!

If you want a hamburger you head to a "Greasy Louie's" and wait for it to be prepared—praying the cook isn't having a bad day. Or, you could go to a hot-dog stand, or a diner like Denny's. Or to plenty of other sit-down restaurants—which cost two, three, or many more times the price of a McDonald's "Happy Meal."

---

[*] Subway has the most outlets—but with lower sales per store.

On top of that, disposable incomes in the 1940s and '50s were a mere quarter what they are today. We could now afford an occasional Big Mac—except there weren't any to be had.

With rare exceptions, most of us would eat at home—just as our parents and grandparents did.

The McDonald brothers proved this. Their new store was in the working class area of San Bernardino, California: before long a major part of their business came from families eating out for the first time.

Ray Kroc and the McDonald brothers changed the way people eat—and revolutionized the restaurant business in the process. "Fast food," as we know it today, simply did not exist on any scale before McDonald's restaurants—and their countless copycats—began appearing across the United States.

Whole Foods and "The Law of Attraction"

Whole Foods was not the world's first organic, environmentally friendly health food store—yet, *it* was the one that changed people's habits.

Founder John Mackey's genius—as we'll see in more detail in Chapter 4—was to create a unique customer experience in the supermarket space. We go to other supermarkets to restock the refrigerator; a Whole Foods store is actually a pleasure to visit, a place to have lunch or just hang out as well as load up your trolley with goodies.

Other health food stores existed to serve the niche market of people who were already sold on the idea of eating "whole foods."

Mackey reached out to "non-foodies" by applying the "law of attraction." Though an evangelist on the subject of eating well (Mackey himself is a vegetarian) by offering a close to full range of foods, including many that a strict health food addict would reject, Whole Foods' "soft sell" approach creates many loyal customers who come for the range, product quality, and ambience—but start to change their diets nonetheless, even if minimally to begin with, thanks to the ease of selecting more healthful foods.

As a result, Whole Foods' success has forced other supermarkets from Safeway and Kroger (and even Walmart) to the corner health food store to alter their product lines.

Which Comes First: the Chicken or the Egg?

Total sales of food products in the US have been rising at around 2% per year. But Whole Foods' organic foods niche between 1996 and 2011 expanded at 18% a year.[11] Is this because Whole Foods and its competitors persuaded people to adopt healthier diets? Or did changing consumer demands drive their growth?

The answer is rarely a simple one.

Steve Jobs built Apple by producing products like the iPod, iPhone, and iPad that nobody knew they wanted until Jobs and his team created them. At the same time, that latent demand had to be there or those product launches would have failed.

The only way to be certain that latent demand exists is to dip your toe in the market. Howard Schultz tested his concept with a small espresso counter in a corner of a Starbucks store when Starbucks was just a coffee roaster. Its success enabled him to gather enough investors to launch *Il Giornale*.

McDonald's originated when Dick and Mac McDonald decided to close their previous business, a "car hop" they started in 1937. It had become a hangout for teenagers, giving it an unsavory reputation with the adult and family market.

Analyzing their business they discovered that 80% of their sales were hamburgers, which spurred them to refurbish their store as a hamburger-only restaurant. Sales and profits were lower to begin with: only after a year did they recover to previous levels—and then accelerate to new heights.

By the time of Ray Kroc's visit, the McDonald brothers had thoroughly tested, refined, and *proven* their concept.

Had that latent consumer demand for Schultz's and the McDonald brothers' tests failed to exist, we would never have heard of either of them.

Only in the case of Walmart does the answer appear clear-cut: few people in this world will turn down the offer of a lower price.

If this is such an obvious business proposition, why didn't stores like Walmart, Kmart and Target emerge years, if not decades earlier?

To be profitable, a discount store must compensate for lower margins with much higher volume. That necessitates a large retail space and a similarly large inventory which, in turn, requires *capital*.

Such a high volume of sales can only be supported by a large customer base, which is easily found in big cities.

But low prices can only be offered profitably if a tight lid is kept on costs, which initially ruled out such high-rent city-center locations.

By the 1950s, the combination of the post-World War II boom and the flight to the suburbs set the scene for a dramatic change in America's retail industry.

The automobile, an essential part of suburban living, meant that large pools of customers were no longer limited to locations served by the fixed mass transit lines of buses and subways. Low-cost out-of-town locations now offered the perfect environment for large discount stores—and entrepreneurs were quick to respond.

Early movers included Ann & Hope (Rhode Island, 1953) and FedMart (San Diego, 1954). Their success inspired a number of clones including Kmart, Target, and Walmart (all started in 1962 within months of each other: March 1, May 1, and July 2 respectively).

In the next chapter we'll see why Walmart, a late-entry "upstart," overtook the first movers in the big-box space, including the better-capitalized Kmart and Target, and changed American shoppers' habits. Walmart lowered the price structure of the American retail industry, saving not just its own customers but *all* retail shoppers untold billions of dollars.

2 *"Most everything I've done I copied from somebody else"*
— Sam Walton[1]

As we've already seen, Starbucks is a "copycat" company, a fusion of an Italian café with a McDonald's-style operating system.

There's nothing wrong with that: most successful businesses are copycats. They're based on the idea that people are much the same the world over. So if people in one part of the world—say, Italy—like sitting around drinking espressos, so will people in another part of the world. Say, the United States.

Or to go one step further—as Starbucks has proved, with stores in 73 countries and counting—*everywhere*.

The genesis of both Starbucks and McDonald's lay in the founder's epiphany: an "Aha!" moment that brought the vision of the business into the founder's mind almost fully formed.

Howard Schultz and Ray Kroc had both the experience to recognize the opportunity, and the talents to turn their vision into a reality.

Clue #2: The Copycat Principle

Starbucks, Ray Kroc's McDonald's, Walmart, and Whole Foods are all *copycats*. None of them were pioneers in their product and market niche; they all took existing practices from their competitors—and *perfected* them.

So are most of the other recent success stories; Internet Explorer copied Netscape. In turn Explorer was copied by Firefox and Google. Samsung copied the iPhone—wherever you look, you'll find copycats.

And being a First Mover can be a disadvantage. Netscape, Burger King, FedMart, Myspace, and Peet's are just a handful of many such examples.

Sam Walton and John Mackey, the founders of Walmart and Whole Foods, had those same talents and experience. But the development of the underlying concepts of these businesses, and their equivalent "Aha!" moments, came more slowly. The slowest of all was Sam Walton's concept for Walmart.

Aside from a stint in the army during World War II, Sam Walton spent his life in the retail business, starting as a management trainee in a J.C. Penney department store in June, 1940.

After the war, he bought a Ben Franklin variety—or five-and-dime—store in Newport, Arkansas. Across the street was another five-and-dime, a Sterling store with twice the sales of his Ben Franklin.

Walton haunted the aisles of the Sterling store to figure out what they were doing that he wasn't.

Which is how much of Walton's, and Walmart's, success began—with his continual study of what *other* retailers were doing. Wherever he travelled he visited retail stores—including, his children recalled, while on vacation. He carried a yellow legal pad (later, a tape recorder as well) and made notes of anything and everything that struck him as a potentially useful idea.

He went to trade association meetings where he picked the brains of other retailers. He visited store owners in other states who were happy to answer his many questions as he was not (then) a competitor.

He returned from every trip with one or more new merchandising, pricing, display, or store-design concepts to try out in his own stores.

He would test each idea in a small and cheap way, discarding it if it failed and rolling it out if it succeeded.

Walton turned "copycatting" into a fine art. His Ben Franklin store soon caught up with and then outsold the Sterling store on the other side of the street.

But one store wasn't enough. By 1960, Walton had grown into the biggest independent store operator in the United States. But "we were doing only $1.4 million [total sales] in fifteen different stores,"[2] most of them Ben Franklins.

He began looking around for something to take him into the next league.

The concept for Walmart developed from a number of sources including:

➤ larger stores—then called family centers—which outsold the combined volume of his fifteen stores in a single location; and,

➤ discount chains like Ann & Hope in New England and FedMart in California, which made up for lower prices with higher volumes.

Walmart was also a *reactive* move on Walton's part. Only when Dallas-based discounter Herb Gibson opened a discount store in Fayetteville, Arkansas, which competed directly with Walton's variety stores, was he spurred into action.

When the first Walmart in Rogers, Arkansas opened on 2 July 1962, it was the laggard of the industry.

It was *not* the first discount store in the state, let alone the country; it was in no sense a dramatically new idea (even the name, Walmart, was a clone of Sol Price's FedMart); and Kmart and Target had beaten Walton to the punch by four and two months, respectively.

No 1962 observer of the retail trade had Walmart on his list of *Retailers Most Likely To Succeed*.

So how did Walmart come from behind, if not from last place, to become the world's #1?

Take the Concept to the Extreme

One reason: with stores in small towns in Arkansas—America's boon-docks—nobody noticed them. Walton could hone his concept while flying under everyone's radar. Even when Walmart went public in 1970, nobody considered it a serious competitor to the then much bigger Kmart and Target chains.

Far more important, Walton took his focus on low prices to an extreme. He insisted on a maximum 30% markup compared to other discounters' up-to-50%.

Costco: Even More Extreme

Costco's markups are even lower than Walmart's: just 14%.[3] Customers make up the difference with membership fees. As you can see from this extract from Costco's financials, without membership fees the company would suffer a loss:

$ million	**2014**	**2013**	**2012**	**2011**	**2010**
Membership fees	2,428	2,286	2,075	1,867	1,691
Net income	2,058	2,039	1,709	1,462	1,303
Membership fees exceed incomte by	**370**	**247**	**366**	**405**	**388**

Source: Costco 2014 Annual Report[4]

To offer the lowest prices *and* make a profit he had to have the lowest costs. A major aspect of the resulting Walmart culture is best expressed in Walton's statement to his buyers: "Every time Walmart spends one dollar foolishly, it comes right out of our customers' pockets. Every time we save them a dollar, that puts us one more step ahead of the competition—which is where we always plan to be."

Walmart has received a lot of flak for allegedly paying its workers less or giving them fewer benefits than its competitors. But that's all part of Walmart's overriding aim: to give every customer the best possible deal by having the lowest-possible costs, across the board.

"I have never seen anything to equal the potential of this place of yours"
—*Ray Kroc to the McDonald brothers*[5]

For seventeen years, Ray Kroc sold paper cups for the Lily-Tulip Cup Company, becoming their star salesman, selling 5 million paper cups a year.

In 1938 he quit Lily-Tulip to start a totally new business selling MultiMixers which made five milkshakes at a time.

Kroc visited thousands of restaurants, soda fountains, dairy bars, and other kitchens across the United States. For most of these customers, one MultiMixer, occasionally two, was more than enough.

But in 1954, he heard of a restaurant in San Bernardino, California called McDonald's that had not two, not three, but *eight* of his MultiMixers—and had just ordered two more. This was something he had to see.

He visited the store on his next trip to Los Angeles—and was astounded. It was a drive-in restaurant and didn't look very impressive—until opening time. Customers parked, ordered from windows and took their purchases back to their cars. There was no seating. Yet, within minutes of the store's 11:00 a.m. opening, the parking lot was nearly full, and long, but fast-moving lines of eager customers were at the windows.

Kroc could see immediately why they needed eight of his MultiMixers: they *had* to make up to forty milkshakes at a time to keep up with demand.

Kroc was impressed with everything he heard and saw. When he went to bed that evening "visions of McDonald's restaurants dotting crossroads all over the country paraded through my brain,"[6] each, of course, with eight of his MultiMixers churning out forty shakes at a time.

At dinner with the McDonald brothers the following evening, he said to them:

> "I have never seen anything to equal the potential of this place of yours. Why don't you open a series of units like this? It would be a gold mine for you and for me, too, because every one would boost my MultiMixer sales. What do you say?"

> Silence.

The brothers weren't interested.

> "It would be a lot of trouble," Dick McDonald objected. "Who could we get to open them for us?"

> I sat there feeling a sense of certitude begin to envelop me. Then I leaned forward and said: "Well, what about me?"[7]

Kroc was then 52 years old, an age when most people are looking forward to retirement. He suffered from diabetes and arthritis, had no gallbladder and not much of his thyroid gland. He returned to Chicago, mulled it over for a week—and returned a week later to sign a franchise.

By 1972 McDonald's, with 2,155 stores, was the world's #1 hamburger chain, a position it has retained, without interruption, to the present day.

The Virtues of Being a Copycat

Being a copycat rather than a pioneer has many virtues. To start with, you know the concept *works*. You don't need to prove that; only whether *you* can make it work in your market.

Burger King

Ray Kroc was not the only person directly inspired by the McDonald brothers.

In 1953—the year *before* Ray Kroc's visit—two men from Jacksonville, Florida, Keith Kramer and Matthew Burns, visited the McDonald brothers' original store.

When they returned home they opened their own copycat named "Burger King" (initially "Insta-Burger King"). It was purchased by its Miami franchisees in 1961.[8]

It's easier to raise capital

The true pioneer must persuade investors that he has the skills, talents, and management team to produce this totally new, untried, and unproven idea at a profit—*and* that consumers will *love* it so much it will fly off the shelves. Easy enough to do in periods like the dot-com boom of the late '90s; not so easy when investors are more rational.

The founder of a copycat company only has to convince investors that he can make money with a proven concept.

You can benefit from the pioneers' experience

One virtue of being a follower is that you don't have to reinvent the wheel. You can (and *should*) learn from other people's successes and mistakes[*], just as Sam Walton did for his entire professional life.

Or, like Ray Kroc, you can take a proven operating system and duplicate it worldwide—with, in Kroc's case, starting further along the learning curve by *not* having to repeat all the McDonald brothers' mistakes.

Or, like Howard Schultz and John Mackey, a combination of both.

You can start with a clean slate

Any company that's been operating for a while establishes a particular way of doing business. Such an institutional legacy—especially when it develops on a catch-as-catch-can basis—can be resistant to change, a perilous attitude in a changing market and when the competition heats up.

With sufficient thought and experiment, you can establish your company's culture and style from day one so that every part of the business meshes with your vision for the company and its primary purpose.

See more at marktier.com/my-books

---

[*] In school, that's called "cheating" and gets you into trouble. In the real world, it's called "market research."

Preview The Winning Investment Habits of Warren Buffett & George Soros

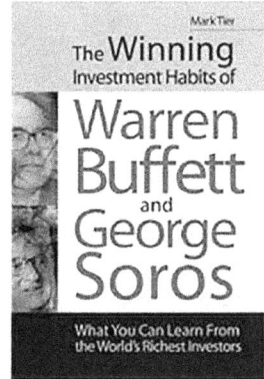

CHAPTER ONE

The Power of Mental Habits

WARREN BUFFETT AND GEORGE SOROS are the world's most successful investors.

Buffett's trademark is buying great businesses for considerably less than what he thinks they're worth — and owning them "forever." Soros is famous for making huge, leveraged trades in the currency and futures markets.

No two investors could seem more different. Their investment methods are as opposite as night and day. On the rare occasions when they bought the same investment, it was for very different reasons.

What could the world's two most successful investors possibly have in common?

On the face of it, not much. But I suspected that if there *is* anything Buffett and Soros *both* do, it could be crucially important...perhaps even the secret behind their success.

The World's 5 Richest Investors

Forbes 2003 Rank	Billionaire	$bn	Source of Wealth	Company/ Country
2	Warren E. Buffett	30.5	Self-made	Berkshire Hathaway, USA
5	Prince Alwaleed Bin Talal Alsaud	17.7	Inherited	Saudi Royal Family, Saudi Arabia
25	Abigail Johnson	8.2	Inherited	Fidelity Investments, USA
38	George Soros	7.0	Self-made	Quantum Funds, USA
39	Khaled, Hayat, Hutham, Lubna & Mary Olayan	6.9	Inherited	Olayan Group, Saudi Arabia

Warren Buffett and George Soros both began with nothing. The other billionaire investors on this list all had a head start.

The more I looked, the more similarities I found. As I analyzed their thinking, how they come to their decisions, and even their beliefs, I found an amazing correspondence. For example:

➤ Buffett and Soros share the same beliefs about the nature of the markets.

➤ When they invest they're not focused on the profits they expect to make. Indeed, they're *not* investing for the money.

➤ Both are far more focused on *not losing* money than on making it.

➤ They *never diversify:* they *always* buy as much of an investment as they can get their hands on.

➤ Their ability to make predictions about the market or the economy has *absolutely nothing* to do with their success.

As I analyzed their beliefs, behaviors, attitudes and decision-making strategies, I found 23 mental habits and strategies they *both* practice religiously. And every one of them is something you can learn.

The Master Investors	
Warren Buffett: *"The Sage of Omaha"*	**George Soros:** *"The Man Who Broke the Bank of England"*
Born 1930, Omaha, Nebraska	Born 1930, Budapest, Hungary
Started managing funds in 1956 with the formation of the Buffett Partnership (dissolved in 1969). Now chairman and major owner, Berkshire Hathaway, Inc.	Began Quantum Fund in 1969 (originally called the Double Eagle Fund). Fund became the Quantum Endowment Fund in 2000.
$1,000 invested with Buffett in 1956 would now be worth $25,289,750.*	$1,000 invested with Soros in 1969 would now be worth $5,142,300.*
Annual compound rate of return: 24.7%	Annual compound rate of return: 28.6%
$1,000 invested in the S&P index in 1956 would now be worth $73,860.*	$1,000 invested in the S&P index in 1969 would now be worth $25,889.*
Number of losing years: 1 (2001) — compared to 13 down years for the S&P 500 since 1956.	Number of losing years: 4 (1981, 1996, 2000, 2002) compared to 9 down years for the S&P 500 since 1969.
* To 31 December 2002.	* To 31 December 2002.

My next step was to "test" these habits against the behavior of other successful investors and commodity traders. The match was perfect.

Peter Lynch, who produced an annual return of 29% during the years he ran the Fidelity Magellan Fund; legendary investors such as Bernard Baruch, Sir John Templeton and Philip Fisher; and every one of dozens of other highly successful investors (*and* commodity traders) I've studied and worked with, all practice exactly the same mental habits as Buffett and Soros, *without exception.*

Cultural background makes no difference. A personally dramatic moment came when I interviewed a Japanese investor living in Hong Kong who trades futures in Singapore, Tokyo and Chicago using Japanese "candlestick" charts. As the conversation proceeded, I checked off one habit after another from my list until I had 22 ticks.

And then he asked whether I thought he was liable for any tax on his profits from trading. That completed the list. (Thanks to Hong Kong's liberal tax regime, it was easy for him to legally do what he wanted: trade tax-free.)

The final test was whether these habits are "portable." Can they be taught? And if you learnt them, would your investment results change for the better?

I started with myself. Since I used to be an investment advisor, and for many years published my own investment newsletter, *World Money Analyst,* it's embarrassing to admit that my own investment results had been dismal. So bad, in fact, that for many years I just let my money sit in the bank.

When I changed my own behavior by adopting these Winning Investment Habits, my investment results improved dramatically. Since 1998 my personal stock market investments have risen an average of 24.4% per year — compared to the S&P which went up only 2.3% per year.* What's more I haven't had a losing year, while the S&P was down three out of those six years. I made more money more easily than I ever thought possible. You can too.

It makes no difference whether you look for stock market bargains like Warren Buffett, trade currency futures like George Soros, use technical analysis, follow "candlestick" charts, buy real estate, buy on dips or buy on breakouts, use a computerized trading system — or just want to salt money away safely for a rainy day. Adopt these habits and your investment returns will soar.

Applying the right mental habits can make the difference between success and failure in anything you do. But the mental strategies of Master

---

* 1 January 1998 to 31 December 2003.

Investors are fairly complex. So let's first look at a simpler example of mental habits.

Why Johnny Can't Spell

Some people are poor spellers. They exasperate their teachers because nothing the teacher does makes any difference to their ability to spell.

So teachers assume the students aren't too bright, even when they display better-than-average intelligence at other tasks — as many do.

The problem isn't a lack of intelligence: it's the *mental strategies* poor spellers use.

Good spellers call up the word they want to spell from memory and *visualize* it. They write the word down by "copying" it from memory. This happens so fast that good spellers are seldom aware of doing it. As with most people who are expert at something, they generally can't explain what they do that makes their success possible...even inevitable.

By contrast, poor spellers spell words by the way they *sound*. That strategy doesn't work very well in English.

The solution is to teach poor spellers to adopt the mental habits of good spellers. As soon as they learn to "look" for the word they want to spell instead of "hearing" it, their spelling problem disappears.

I was amazed the first time I showed a poor speller this strategy. The man, a brilliant writer, had gotten a string of Bs in school all with the comment: "You'd have gotten an A if only you'd learn how to spell!"

In less than five minutes, he was spelling words like "antidisestablish-mentarianism," "rhetoric" and "rhythm," which had confounded him all his life. He already knew what they looked like; he just didn't know that he had to look!*

Such is the power of mental habits.

The Structure of Mental Habits

A habit is a learned response that has become automatic through repetition. Once ingrained, the mental processes by which a habit operates are primarily *subconscious.*

This is clearly true of the good speller: he is completely unaware of *how* he spells a word correctly. He just "knows" that it's right.

But doesn't most of what the successful investor does take place at the conscious level? Aren't reading annual reports, analyzing balance sheets,

---

* The Spelling Strategy was developed by Robert Dilts, co-developer of the branch of applied psychology known as Neuro-Linguistic Programming.

even detecting patterns in charts of stock or commodity prices conscious activities?

To an extent, yes. But consciousness is only the tip of the mental iceberg. Behind every conscious thought, decision or action is a complex array of subconscious mental processes — not to mention hidden beliefs and emotions that can sabotage even the most determined person.

For example, if someone's been told "You can't spell" over and over again, that belief can become part of his identity. He can understand the good speller's strategy, and with an instructor's guidance can even replicate the good speller's results. But left to his own devices, he quickly reverts to his old mental pattern.

Only by changing the belief that "I am a poor speller" can he adopt the good speller's mental habits.

Another, though usually minor, stumbling block is the lack of an associated skill. A tiny percentage of people simply can't create an internal mental image: they have to be taught how to visualize before they can become good spellers.

Four elements are needed to sustain a mental habit:

1. a belief that drives your behavior;

2. a mental strategy — a series of internal conscious and subconscious processes;

3. a sustaining emotion; and

4. associated skills.

Let's apply this structure to analyze another process, one that's simpler than the habits of highly successful investors but more complex than the "Spelling Strategy."

"IceBreakers"

Imagine we're at a party and we see two men eyeing the same attractive woman. As we watch, we notice that the first man starts to walk towards her but then stops, turns, heads over to the bar, and spends the rest of the evening being an increasingly drunken wallflower. A few moments later, we see the second man walk over to the woman and begin talking with her.

A while later we become aware that the second man seems to be talking to just about everybody at the party. Eventually, he comes over to us and initiates a conversation. We conclude that he's a really nice guy, but when we think about it later we realize he didn't say very much at all: we did most of the talking.

We all know people like this, who can walk up to a total stranger and in a few minutes be chatting away like they're lifelong friends. I call them "IceBreakers," and behind their behavior is the mental habits they practice:

1. *Belief:* They believe that *everybody* is interesting.

2. *Mental Strategy:* They hear their own voice inside their head saying: "Isn't he/she an interesting person."

3. *Sustaining Emotion:* They feel curious, even excited, at the prospect of meeting somebody new. They feel good about themselves, and their attention is focused externally. (If they're preoccupied with some problem or feeling depressed about something — internally focused — they won't be "in the mood" for conversation.)

4. *Associated Skills:* They establish rapport by making eye contact and smiling with their eyes. When they have a sense of rapport, they initiate a conversation with some innocuous remark, and maintain it by listening rather than talking, keeping eye contact and focusing their attention on the person (giving that person a sense of importance), and by wondering what's going on in this person's mind.

You can get a taste of how this works by trying it out for yourself. Just imagine (if you don't already believe it) that you consider *all* people are interesting; and hear your own voice saying, "Isn't he/she an interesting person." Then look around, and if you're alone imagine that you're in the middle of a crowd. You should be able to feel the difference (if only for a moment).

The Wallflower, who ended up at the bar, had a very different mental strategy. After an initial flash of interest, he "ran a movie" in his head of all the times he had been hurt in a relationship, felt lousy — and went to have a beer to drown his sorrows. His emotional reaction was the expression of a subconscious, self-limiting belief that "I'm not good enough," or "I always get hurt in relationships."

Another pattern when meeting someone new is to continually wonder: "*Is* this person interesting (to *me*)?" This "Self-Centered" approach reflects a belief that only *some* people are interesting. And it has very different behavioral consequences.

On the next page is a chart of these three different mental habits.

The Wallflower or the Self-Centered person can easily learn all the IceBreaker's skills: how to establish rapport, how to "smile with your eyes," how to be a good listener and so on. He can even create an internal voice saying, "Isn't he/she an interesting person."

	IceBreaker	Wallflower*	Self-Centered
Belief	People are . interesting	I'm not good enough/ I always get hurt.	Some people are interesting.
Mental Strategy	*Internal voice:* "Isn't he/she an interesting person."	Recall previous relationships.	*Internal voice:* "*Is* this person interesting (to *me*)?"
Mental Focus	External	Internal	Primarily internal
Emotion	Curiosity, excitement	Hurt	Uncertainty
Skills	Rapport, good listener	N/A	Questioning

*Note: this is only one of many variants of what we might call "Wallflower Strategies."

But what happens when the Wallflower actually tries to initiate a conversation with a complete stranger? His self-limiting beliefs override his conscious attempt to do something different — and nothing happens.

In the same way, an investor who subconsciously believes that "I don't deserve to make money" or "I'm a loser" cannot succeed in the markets no matter how many skills he learns or how hard he tries.

There are similar kinds of beliefs that lie behind many investors' losses, beliefs that I call *The Seven Deadly Investment Sins...*

Continue at marktier.com/7sins

Other Titles by Mark Tier

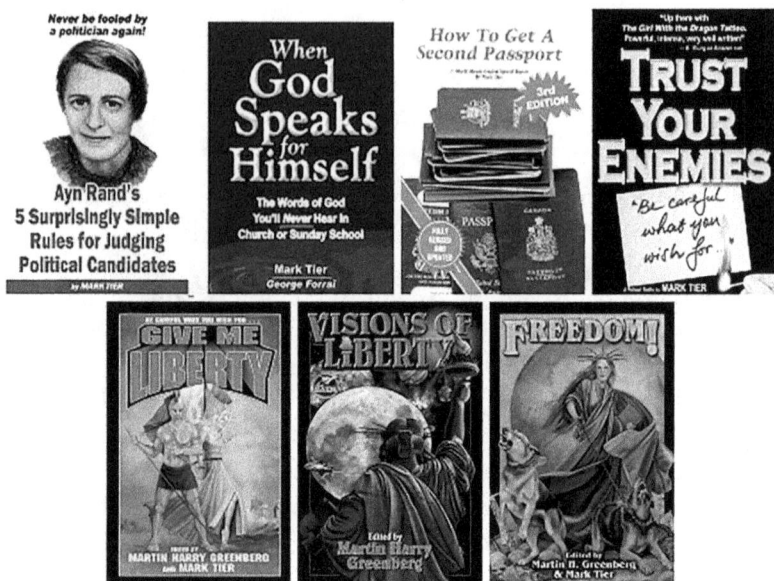

See more at marktier.com/my-books

www.ingramcontent.com/pod-product-compliance
Lightning Source LLC
Chambersburg PA
CBHW061049220326
41597CB00018BA/2699